THE
MOTHER'S
TREASURY

DORLING KINDERSLEY
London • New York • Sydney
www.dk.com

A DORLING KINDERSLEY BOOK
www.dk.com

Editor   Caroline Hunt
Art Editor   Dawn Terrey
Senior Editor   David Pickering
Senior Managing Editor   Anna Kruger
Picture Researcher   Jo Walton
Production Controller   Louise Daly
DTP Designer   Robert Campbell
U.S. Editor   Claudia Volkman
U.S. Art Director   Gloria Chantell

First published in Great Britain in 2000
by Dorling Kindersley Limited,
9 Henrietta Street, London WC2E 8PS

A CIP catalogue record for this book is available from the British Library.

ISBN 0-7513-7271-4
Colour reproduction in Italy by GRB editrice srl
Printed and bound in Hong Kong by Imago

CONTENTS

6   Hans Tichy *Mrs. Masari and Her Daughter*

THE
MOTHER'S
TREASURY

Presented to

_____

_____

INTRODUCTION

Motherhood is both an incredible privilege and a great responsibility. Being a mother calls forth the best of a woman's gifts and abilities. With the birth of a child, a woman begins a journey full of rich joys and unexpected challenges, as well as great rewards.

With all the choices facing women today, motherhood remains a high calling. A mother's love, after all, is true, deep, and pure – a visible example of God's own love.

Whether you are expecting your first baby soon or have years of experience as a mother, this special collection of inspiring quotes, Scripture verses, and timeless artwork is designed to remind you of the blessings of motherhood.

THE
BLESSINGS
OF A CHILD

The tie which links mother and child is of
such pure and immaculate strength as to be
never violated. Holy, simple, and beautiful in
its construction, it is the emblem of all we can
imagine of fidelity and truth.

WASHINGTON IRVING

Mary Cassatt *Maternal Caress*

Behold, children are a heritage
from the Lord.

PSALM 127:3 (NKJV)

Children are not our properties
to own or rule over, but gifts to cherish and
care for. Our children are our most important
guests, who enter into our home, ask for
careful attention, stay for a while, and then
leave to follow their own way.

HENRI NOUWEN

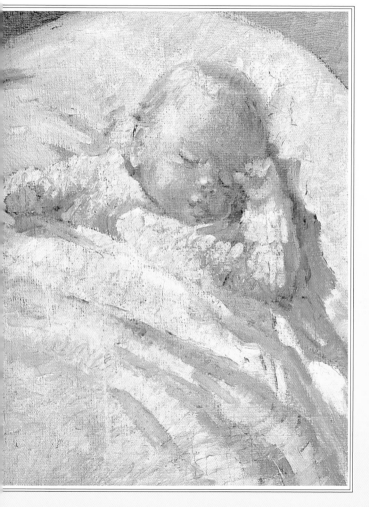

Dorothea Sharp *A Sleeping Baby*   11

Mary Cassatt *Mother, Sara, and the Baby*

For you created my inmost being; you knit
me together in my mother's womb. I praise
you because I am fearfully and wonderfully
made ... All the days ordained for me were
written in your book before one of them
came to be.

PSALM 139:13, 16 (NIV)

Did I conceive a child? or, child,
by forming did you conceive a mother?

CAROL VAN KLOMPENBURG

Children are the hands by which
we take hold of heaven.

HENRY WARD BEECHER

God sends children for another purpose
than merely to keep up the race – to enlarge our
hearts; to make us unselfish and full of kindly
sympathies and affections; to give our souls
higher aims and to call out all our faculties;
to extend enterprise and exertion....
My soul blesses the great Father every day that he
has gladdened the earth with little children.

MARY HEWITT

Joaquin y Bastida Sorolla *Children in the Sea*   15

Joaquin y Bastida Sorolla *Mother*

In the sheltered
simplicity of the first
days after a baby is
born, one sees again
the magical closed
circle, the miraculous
sense of two people
existing only for each
other, the tranquil sky
reflected on the face
of the mother nursing
her child.

ANNE MORROW
LINDBERGH

Children are God's apostles,

day by day sent forth to preach

of love, and hope, and peace.

JAMES RUSSELL LOWELL

Jesus called the children to him

and said, "Let the little children come to me,

and do not hinder them, for the kingdom

of God belongs to such as these."

LUKE 18:16 (NIV)

Dorothea Sharp *Children on the Seashore*   19

Dorothea Sharp *Picking Flowers*

A rose can say I love you,

Orchids can enthrall,

But a weed bouquet in a chubby fist,

Oh my, that says it all.

AUTHOR UNKNOWN

God blesses those who are gentle

and lowly, for the whole earth

will belong to them.

MATTHEW 5:5 (NLT)

A
MOTHER'S
ROLE

Parenthood is partnership with God.
You are not moulding iron nor chiselling
marble; you are working with the Creator
of the universe in shaping human
character and determining destiny.

RUTH VAUGHN

As a mother comforts her child,

so I will comfort you.

ISAIAH 66:13 (NRSV)

They always looked back before turning
the corner, for their mother was always at the
window to nod and smile, and wave her hand at
them. Somehow it seemed as if they couldn't have
got through the day without that, for whatever their
mood might be, the last glimpse of that motherly
face was sure to affect them like sunshine.

LOUISA MAY ALCOTT, *LITTLE WOMEN*

Ferdinand Georg *Young Farmer's Wife with Her Three Children at the Window*   25

Gaetano Chierici *Feeding the Baby*

Nobody knows of the work it makes

to keep the home together,

Nobody knows of the steps it takes,

Nobody knows – but mother.

AUTHOR UNKNOWN

My mother was the source from which I
derived the guiding principles of my life.

JOHN WESLEY

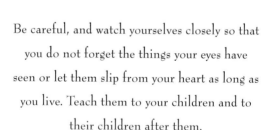

Be careful, and watch yourselves closely so that
you do not forget the things your eyes have
seen or let them slip from your heart as long as
you live. Teach them to your children and to
their children after them.

DEUTERONOMY 4:9 (NIV)

Seymour Joseph Guy *Knowledge Is Power*

Alberto Bribiesca *The Alms Giver*

My child, if you accept my words and treasure
up my commandments within you ... then you will
understand righteousness and justice and equity,
every good path; for wisdom will come into
your heart and knowledge will be pleasant to
your soul; prudence will watch over you; and
understanding will guard you.

PROVERBS 2:1, 9-11 (NRSV)

Virtue is the health of the soul.
It gives a flavour to the smallest
leaves of life.

JOHN JOUBERT

Every mother has the breathtaking
privilege of sharing with God in the creation of
new life. She helps bring into existence a soul
that will endure for all eternity.

JAMES KELLER

For I am confident of this very thing,
that He who began a good work in you will perfect
it until the day of Christ Jesus.

PHILIPPIANS 1:6 (NASB)

Mary Cassatt *The Mother's Kiss*

34   Auguste Renoir *The Afternoon of the Children in Wargemont*

Unless the Lord
builds a house, the work
of the builders is useless.
It is useless for you to
work so hard from early
morning until late at
night, anxiously working
for food to eat; for
God gives rest to his
loved ones.

PSALM 127:1-2 (NLT)

The history of humanity
is not the history of its
wars, but the history of
its households.

JOHN RUSKIN

CELEBRATE
THE
MOMENT

Line by line, moment by moment,
special times are etched into our
memories in the permanent ink of
everlasting love in our relationships.

GLORIA GAITHER

Dorothea Sharp *Baby Picking Daisies*   37

Look at all those children! There they sit around
your table as vigorous and healthy as young olive
trees. That is the Lord's reward for those who fear
him. May the Lord continually bless you from Zion.
May you see Jerusalem prosper as long as you live.
May you live to enjoy your grandchildren.
And may Israel have quietness and peace.

PSALM 128:3-6 (NLT)

Do not delay; the golden memories fly!

HENRY WADSWORTH LONGFELLOW

Grandchildren are the crown of the aged,

and the glory of children is

their parents.

PROVERBS 17:6 (NRSV)

Mary Cassatt *Grandmother Reading to Children*

40   Peder Severin Kroyer *"Hip Hip Hurrah!"* Artists' Party

Go and celebrate
with a feast of choice
foods and sweet drinks,
and share gifts of food
with people who have
nothing prepared.
This is a sacred day
before our Lord. Don't
be dejected and sad, for
the joy of the Lord is
your strength!

NEHEMIAH 8:10 (NLT)

41

If a blade of grass can grow in a concrete
walk and a fig tree in the side of the mountain cliff,
a human being empowered with an invincible faith
can survive all odds the world can throw against
his tortured soul.

ROBERT SCHULLER

It is the heart which is aware of God,
and not reason. That is what faith is:
God perceived intuitively by the heart,
not by reason.

MALCOLM MUGGERIDGE

Emile Claus *In Flanders*

Happy times and
bygone days are never
lost ... in truth, they
grow more wonderful
within the heart that
keeps them.

KAY ANDREW

I have no greater joy
than to hear that my
children walk in
truth.

3 JOHN 4 (KJV)

Emile Cagniart *Going for a Paddle* 45

46   Mary Cassatt *Mother Louise Holding Up Her Blue-Eyed Child*

We have only this moment, sparkling
like a star in our hand – and melting
like a snowflake.

MARIE BEYNON RAY

There is a time for everything,

a season for every activity under heaven.

A time to be born and a time to die.

A time to plant and a time to harvest....

A time to cry and a time to laugh.

A time to grieve and a time to dance....

A time to keep and a time to throw away....

A time to be quiet and a time to speak up.

A time to love and a time to hate.

A time for war and a time for peace.

ECCLESIASTES 3:1-2, 4, 6-8 (NLT)

Every day in a life fills the whole

life with expectations and memories.

C.S. LEWIS

George Smith *Musing on the Future*

Auguste Renoir *Gabrielle and Coco*

To be grateful is to recognize the love
of God in everything he has given us —
and he has given us everything.
Every breath we draw is a gift of his love, every
moment of existence, a gift of grace.

THOMAS MERTON

Every good and perfect gift is
from above, coming down from the
Father of the heavenly lights.

JAMES 1:17 (NIV)

A
MOTHER'S
CHARACTER

The people who influence us most are not those
who buttonhole us and talk to us, but those who
live their lives like the stars in heaven and the
lilies in the field, perfectly simply, and
unaffectedly. Those are the lives that mould us.

OSWALD CHAMBERS

You are the light of the world – like a city on a mountain, glowing in the night for all to see. Don't hide your light under a basket! Instead, put it on a stand and let it shine for all. In the same way, let your good deeds shine out for all to see, so that everyone will praise your heavenly Father.

MATTHEW 5:14-16 (NLT)

Now you are full of light from the Lord, and your behavior should show it! For this light within you produces only what is good and right and true.

EPHESIANS 5:8-9 (NLT)

Bertha Wegmann *A Mother and Daughter in an Interior*   55

Mary Cassatt *Mother About to Wash Her Sleepy Child*

A contented woman has a healthy,
balanced view of God that enhances her value
in the church and in society. She isn't perfect,
but her deep relationship with God has
transformed her pain and personality.
In the freedom of his love, she has discovered
her uniqueness and is eager to follow his
direction for living in this world.

DR. DEBORAH NEWMAN

No man is poor who had a godly mother.

ABRAHAM LINCOLN

You have a unique message to deliver, a unique
song to sing, a unique act of love to bestow.
This message, this song, and this act of love
have been entrusted exclusively to
the one and only you.

JOHN POWELL

Live a life filled with love for others.

EPHESIANS 5:2 (NLT)

Dorothea Sharp *The Ball of Wool*

F. W. Bourdillon *Jubilee Hat*

Be kind to one another, tenderhearted,

forgiving one another,

just as God in Christ forgave you.

EPHESIANS 4:32 (NKJV)

Kind words can be short and easy to speak,

but their echoes are truly endless.

MOTHER TERESA

Her chubby hands crept round my neck

And whispered words I can't forget,

They cast a light upon my soul –

On secrets no one knew.

They startled me, I hear them yet:

"Someday I'll be like you!"

AUTHOR UNKNOWN

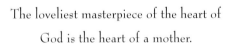

The loveliest masterpiece of the heart of

God is the heart of a mother.

THÉRÈSE OF LISIEUX

Mary Cassatt *Maternal Kiss*

64   Berthe Morisot *Woman and Child in a Garden at Bougival*

Let your prayer be that God's goodness and
the joy of Christ will shine through your life
in such a way that your children will see
the reality of your personal relationship
with the Almighty God.

DR. KEVIN LEMAN

It is only with gratitude that life
becomes rich.

DIETRICH BONHOEFFER

A
TIME
TO REFLECT

Practise the art of aloneness and you will
discover the treasure of tranquillity.
Develop the art of solitude and you will
unearth the gift of serenity.

WILLIAM WARD

Valentin Aleksandrovich Serov *Girl with Peaches*

It requires a lot of inner solitude and silence to
become aware of the gentle movements of the Spirit
of God within me. God does not shout, scream, or
push. The Spirit of God is soft and gentle like a
small voice or a light breeze. It is the spirit of love.

HENRI NOUWEN

We need time to dream,
time to remember,
time to reach the infinite.
Time to be.

GLADYS TABER

We need to find God,
and he cannot be
found in noise and
restlessness. God is
the friend of silence.

MOTHER TERESA

Be still and know
that I am God.

PSALM 46:10 (NIV)

Vilhelm Hammershoi *A Woman Sewing in an Interior*   71

It is in lonely solitude that God delivers his
best thoughts, and the mind needs to be still
and quiet to receive them.

CHARLES SWINDOLL

Every woman battles with the whirl of
busyness and can benefit from holding her own
restoration time with God.

PEGGY GRANT

Walter Langley *Tender Grace of a Day That Is Dead*   73

Hans Tichy *Mrs. Masari and Her Daughter*

Peace I leave with you, my peace
I give unto you: not as the world giveth,
give I unto you.
Let not your heart be troubled,
neither let it be afraid.

JOHN 14:27 (KJV)

You alone, O Lord,
make me dwell in safety.

PSALM 4:8 (NKJV)

Hans Heyerdahl *At the Window*

Teach me your way, O Lord, and I will walk in
your truth; give me an undivided heart, that I may
fear your name. I will praise you, O Lord my God,
with all my heart; I will glorify your
name forever. For great is your love toward me.

PSALM 86:11-13 (NIV)

You made us for yourself, O God,
and our hearts are restless until they rest in you.

AUGUSTINE

Lord, my heart is not haughty, nor my eyes
lofty. Neither do I concern myself with great
matters, nor with things too profound for me.
Surely I have calmed and quieted my soul,
like a weaned child with his mother; like a
weaned child is my soul within me.

PSALM 131:1-2 (NKJV)

Before me,
even as behind,
God is – and all is well.

JOHN GREENLEAF WHITTIER

Victor Lecomte *A Private Moment*   79

A
LASTING
LEGACY

The home should be a self-contained shelter of
security; a kind of school where life's basic lessons
are taught; and a kind of church where God is
honoured; a place where wholesome recreation and
simple pleasures are enjoyed.

BILLY GRAHAM

Knut Ekvall *The Reading Lesson*

We can't create our daughters' faith for them,
but we can give our daughters a remarkable
range of spiritual strategies for confronting and
coping with life's challenges. We can't totally
predict the final outcome of our long years of
mothering, but we can point and guide our
daughters in the right direction.

DEBRA EVANS

Future generations will also serve him.
Our children will hear about the
wonders of the Lord.

PSALM 22:30 (NLT)

Sir George Clausen *French Peasant Girls Praying*   83

I long to put the
experience of fifty
years at once into
your young lives,
to give you at once
the key of that
treasure chamber
every gem of which
has cost me tears
and struggles and
prayers, but you
must work for these
inward treasures
yourselves.

HARRIET BEECHER
STOWE

Rudolf Hausleithner von Gemälde *Family Scene*   85

Valentin Aleksandrovich Serov *Two Boys*

We do not understand the intricate pattern
of the stars in their course, but we know that
he who created them does, and that just as
surely as he guides them, he is charting a
safe course for us.

BILLY GRAHAM

There is nothing but God's grace.
We walk upon it; we breathe it;
we live and die by it.

ROBERT LOUIS STEVENSON

Your children must know that your love is
forever, whenever, and with no strings attached.

MARY LaGRAND BOUMA

Now these three remain: faith, hope, and love.
But the greatest of these is love.

1 CORINTHIANS 13:13 (NIV)

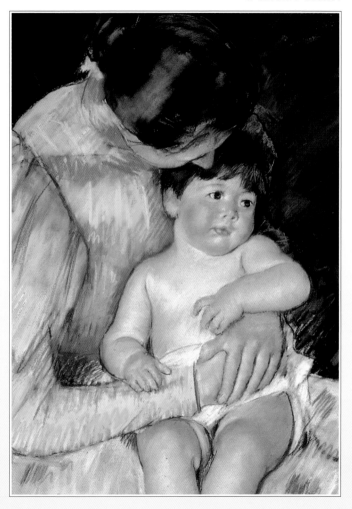

Mary Cassatt *Mother and Child*   89

Remember you are very special to God as his
precious child. He has promised to complete
the good work he has begun in you. As you
continue to grow in him, he will teach you to
be a blessing to others.

GARY SMALLEY AND JOHN TRENT

We know that God causes everything to
work together for the good of those who
love God and are called according
to his purpose for them.

ROMANS 8:28 (NLT)

Dorothea Sharp *An Afternoon Walk*

Mary Cassatt *Mother and Child*

You will find, as you look
back on your life, that the moments
when you have really lived are the moments
when you have done
things in the spirit of love.

HENRY DRUMMOND

The secret of life is that all we have
and are is a gift of grace to be shared.

LLOYD JOHN OGILVIE

MY OWN REFLECTIONS

_____

_____

_____

_____

_____

_____

_____

_____

_____

ACKNOWLEDGMENTS

The publisher would like to thank the following for their kind permission to reproduce their photographs:

AKG London: 67; Neideroesterr. Landesmuseum, Vienna 84-85; SMPK Nationalgalerie, Berlin 34-35, 87; SMPK Artothek: Christie's, New York 12, 18, 26, 29, 37, 42, 61, 80; Neue Pinakothek, Munchen 25. Bridgeman Art Library, London/New York: Bonhams, London UK: 10-11; Bristol City Museum and Art Gallery, UK 9, 50; Brodski Museum, St. Petersburg, Russia 66; Christie's Images, London UK 70-71; John Davies Fine Painting; John Davies Fine Paintings, Stow-on-the-Wold, Glos, UK 3, 36, 59, 91; Los Angeles County Museum of Art CA 56; Mallett and Son Antiques Ltd, London, UK 23, 49; Museo d'Arte Moderna, Venice, Italy 52; Museo Sorolla, Madrid/Index 15, 16-17; Nasjonalgalleriet, Oslo, Norway 76; National Museum and Gallery of Wales, Cardiff 64-65; Oldham Art Gallery, Lancashire, UK 73; Private Collection/Giraudon 92; Private Collection 6, 60, 74; Private Collection, NY, USA 39; State Russian Museum, St. Petersburg 86; Tretyakov Gallery, Moscow 27, 68; Victoria and Albert Museum, London 32, 83; Whitford and Hughes, London, UK 19, 20-21, 77, 81; Christie's Images Ltd 1999: 8, 13, 22-23, 46, 47, 53, 55, 72, 89; Edimedia: Christies Images 33; E.T. Archive: Queretera Museum, Mexico 30; Fine Art Photographic Library Ltd: Galerie Berko 43, 44-45, 90; Private Collection 40-41; Waterhouse and Dodd 79c; Philadelphia Museum Of Art, Bequest of Anne Hinchman: 63, cover.